Suzuki

VIOLA SCHOOL

Volume 5
Viola Part
Revised Edition

ISBN 0-87487-249-9

ACKNOWLEDGMENTS

The compositions in this volume were arranged for viola and piano by Doris Preucil. The viola parts were edited by William and Doris Preucil with the assistance of Suzuki Association of America Viola Committee members Leroy Bauer, Louita Clothier, William Foster, Virginia Schneider, and Elizabeth Stuen-Walker.

INTRODUCTION

FOR THE STUDENT: This material is part of the worldwide Suzuki Method® of teaching. The companion recording should be used along with this publication. A piano accompaniment book is also available for this material.

FOR THE TEACHER: In order to be an effective Suzuki teacher, ongoing education is encouraged. Each regional Suzuki association provides teacher development for its membership via conferences, institutes, short-term and long-term programs. In order to remain current, you are encouraged to become a member of your regional Suzuki association, and if not already included, the International Suzuki Association.

FOR THE PARENT: Credentials are essential for any teacher you choose. We recommend you ask your teacher for his or her credentials, especially those relating to training in the Suzuki Method®. The Suzuki Method® experience should foster a positive relationship among the teacher, parent and child. Choosing the right teacher is of the utmost importance.

To obtain more information about the Suzuki Association in your region, please contact:

International Suzuki Association
www.internationalsuzuki.org

CONTENTS

Tonalization

Tonalization exercises should be practiced at each lesson.
Exercise for beautiful tone and vibrato.

Exercise for *Forte* and *Piano*

1. For *forte*: Place the bow near the bridge (B) and use a whole, straight bow.

2. For *piano*: Place the bow away from the bridge (A) and use a whole, straight bow.

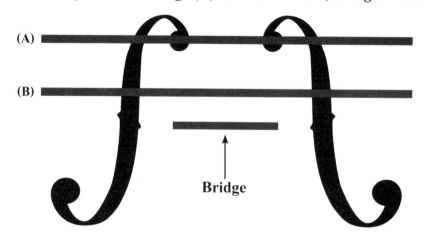

Bridge

Position Etudes – 5th Position

The indication  **means that pupils should first play** ... **and then** ...

A string:

The first finger should always stay down in such practice.
Try stopped bows on the slurs at first.

When this exercise is mastered on one string, practice on the next string.
Position practice should always be done by memory.

Please review Etudes for 2nd, 3rd, and 4th position in Suzuki Viola Volumes 3
and 4.

Etude for Changing Strings

Try to maintain a constant tone and tempo, taking care not to get too fast.

Bowing variants:

1
Sonata in G Major

B. Marcello
Realized and edited by Doris Preucil

2 Country Dance

C. M. von Weber

(Nina)

10

Numbers refer to circled numbers in music.

Keep 1st finger down.

Play with separate bows first.

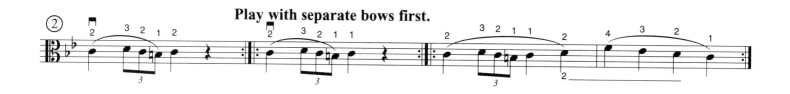

Listen for clear tone on 4th finger.

**Bow should settle firmly on string
before beginning up -bow.**

3 Nina

G. B. Pergolesi

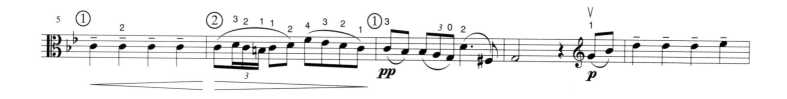

Circled numbers refer to corresponding numbers in practice suggestions.

4
Spinning Wheel

N. Rubinstein

⑤ Gigue

Allegro vivace

F. M. Veracini

Exercises for Shaping the Left Hand*

① **Place 1st finger as indicated. Touch first finger to neck without gripping.**

② **As the pitch of the 3rd or 4th finger is the same as, or an octave from its neighboring string, produce the same pitch by listening for resonance. Do not use vibrato so that the resonance can easily be heard. Keep fingers from touching neighboring strings to allow the resonance to sound.**

③ **Observe carefully the form of the hand and fingers.**

Repeat many times.
Also play this finger pattern
on the D, G, and C strings.

*From Suzuki Violin School Quint Etudes.

④ **Test for exact pitch of the 4th finger. Also practice this starting on the D and G strings.**

⑤ **Second Position**

⑥ **Third Position**

⑦ **On one string**

**The downward shift of the
left hand will be difficult
if the viola is not held properly.**

6 Suite I in G major
Prelude

Johann Sebastian Bach

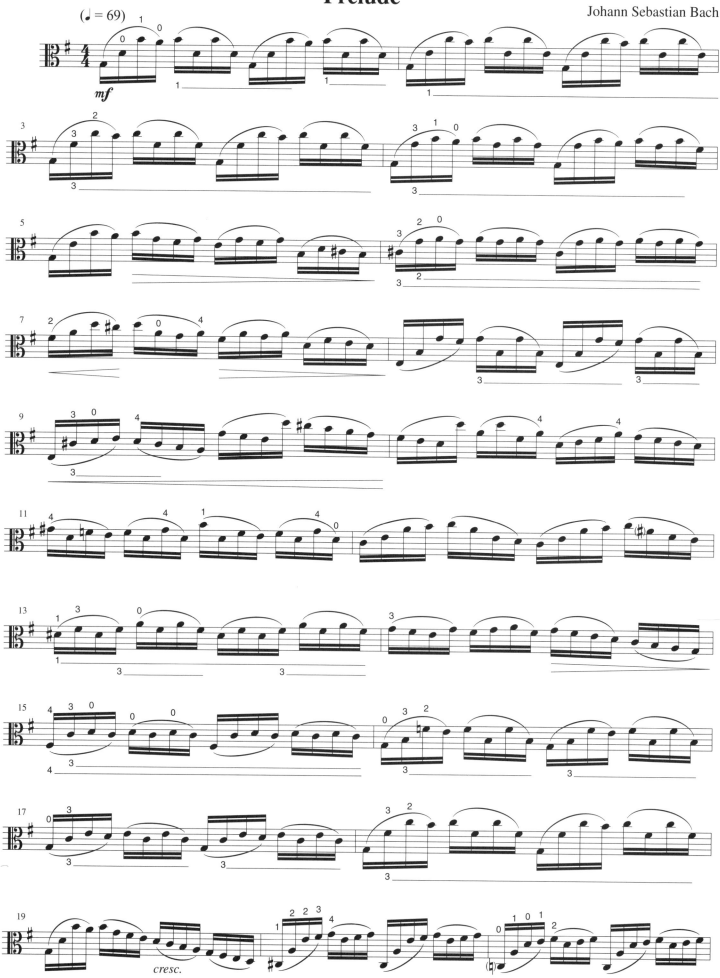

19

Courante

Gigue

7
Moto Perpetuo*

C. Bohm

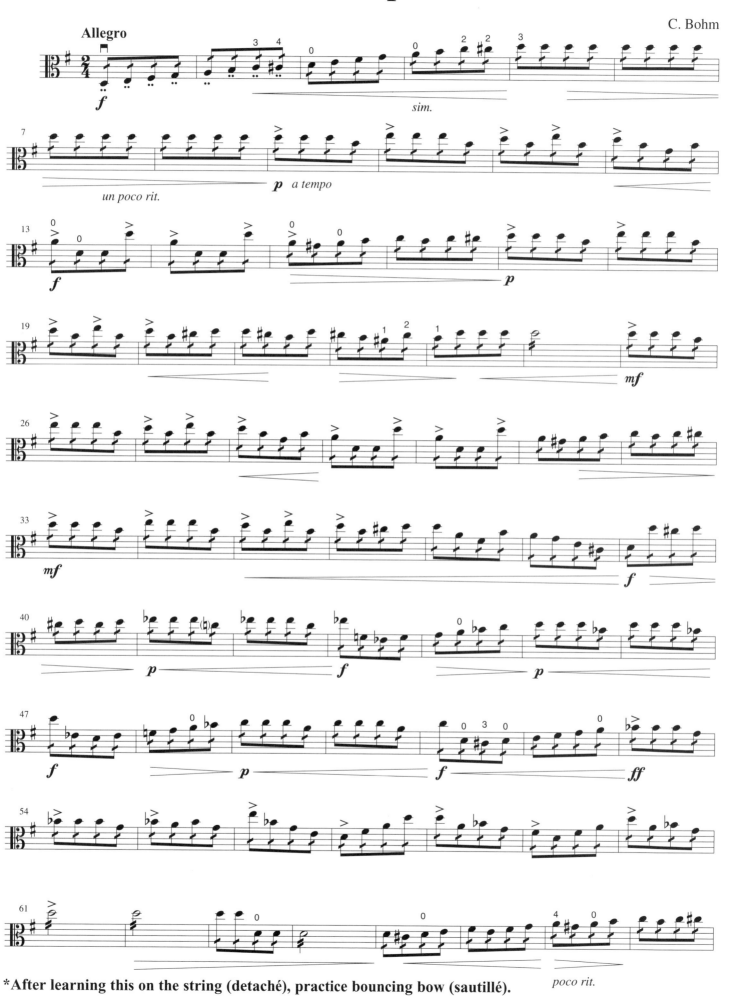

*After learning this on the string (detaché), practice bouncing bow (sautillé). *poco rit.*

8 Old French Dances
I. L'Agréable

M. Marais

*Slight retake

II. La Provençale

III. La Matelotte

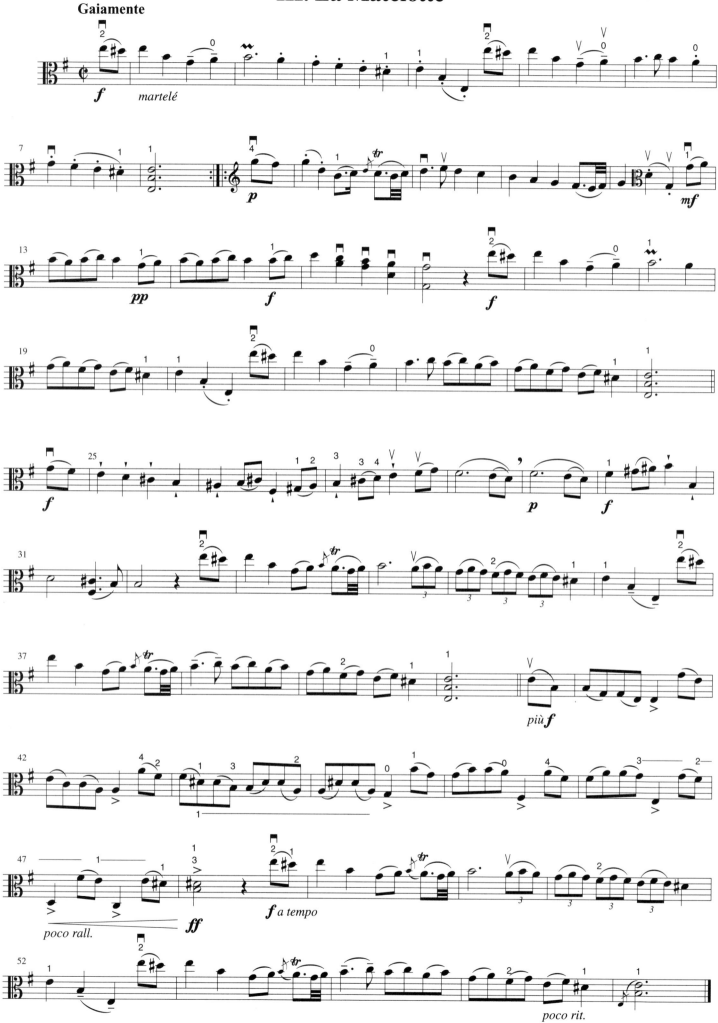

IV. Le Basque

Tonalization

Use full bows with smooth bow and string changes.

   I - A string
  II - D string
 III - G string
 IV - C string

C Major Scale – 3 octaves

C Minor Scale – (melodic)

C Major Arpeggio

C Minor Arpeggio

Shifting Studies

1) **Practice each exercise with the various finger combinations indicated.**
2) **Practice without vibrato, then with vibrato.**
3) **Also practice using dotted rhythm** (♪. ♪ ♪. ♪)
4) **After learning these studies on the A string, transpose to the other strings.**

```
a) 1  1  1  1    1  1  1  1   sim.
b) 1  2  2  1    1  2  2  1   sim.
c) 1  2  2  1    1  3  3  1    1  3  3  1   sim.
d) 1  2  2  1    1  3  3  1    1  4  4  1    1  4  4  1   sim.
```

```
a) 2  2  2  2   sim.
b) 2  1  1  2    2  1   sim.
c) 2  3  3  2    2  3  3  2   sim.
d) 2  3  3  2    2  4  4  2    2  4   sim.
```

```
a) 3  3  3  3   sim.
b) 3  4  4  3    3  4  4  3   sim.
c) 3  2  2  3    3  2  2  3   sim.
d) 3  1  1  3    3  1  1  3   sim.
```

```
a) 4  4  4  4   sim.
b) 4  3  3  4    4  3  3  4   sim.
c) 4  2  2  4    4  2  2  4   sim.
d) 4  1  1  4    4  1  1  4   sim.
```

Always shift on the finger last used.

rays shift on the finger last used.

9 Concerto No. 3 in C Minor

F. Seitz
arr. D. Preucil

Allegro risoluto